Brother Lawrence for today

CLOSER
THAN A
BROTHER

DAVID WINTER

Harold Shaw Publishers
Wheaton, Illinois

CONTENTS

INTRODUCTION

Nicholas Herman was born in 1611 in France, of humble parents. He had an experience of conversion at the age of eighteen, and after some years as a soldier and then as a footman, entered a lay community of Carmelites at Paris, where he took the name Brother Lawrence. He died at the age of eighty in 1691.

During the twenty-five years he spent in the community he served in various menial roles, mostly in the hospital kitchen, but he became known within and beyond the Carmelites for his quite remarkable and serene faith, and his simple but dynamic experience of "the presence of God." Although he was a comparatively uneducated layman, Brother Lawrence received many letters and other requests from Christians anxious to find a similar reality and confidence in their own spiritual lives. Even bishops and other church dignitaries turned to him with problems and doubts about their faith.

To all, Brother Lawrence gave the same answers: stop putting your trust in human rules, devotional exercises and acts of penance. Instead, exercise a living, obedient faith in God. Live as though he were beside you and with you all the time—*as indeed he is.* Seek to do what he wants, as and when he commands it, and make his command your joy and chief pleasure. The man who lives like that will be fully human, completely Christian and genuinely happy.

Of course, Brother Lawrence had his critics, both inside and outside the Community. Some felt he was pretending to a knowledge of God not available to ordinary people. Others saw his claims to extraordinary delights and raptures from God's presence as affronts to sober faith and reverence.

But the testimony of those who knew him was that here was a man who walked with God. Brother Lawrence, like few men since Bible times, it would seem, had found—or been shown—the secret of a happy, holy relationship with God. Certainly *The Practice of the Presence of God*—the title given to the collection of his "conversations" and "letters"—has to be included in any list of the really great devotional books of the Christian religion.

However, like many other great but ancient

books, it poses enormous problems for the modern reader. The stilted eighteenth-century English of most of the available translations does nothing to make the thoughts of a seventeenth-century Frenchman relevant or dynamic to twentieth-century Christians, and the whole setting of his life and times serves to heighten the sense of remoteness from our present-day tensions and problems.

And yet I believe Brother Lawrence has a message of startling relevance to modern Christians. After all, the modern world makes it harder and harder to live a "spiritual" life. All around us a dehumanizing process is at work: machines replacing hands, computers replacing minds, psychotherapy replacing prayer. And while these things are not bad in themselves, taken together with the accelerating advance of science, the turbulent tempo of life and the external tensions of events, they have conspired to produce a society which has little time for humanity and even less for God. So how does a twentieth-century Christian set about living the Christian life in this sort of situation? How can we be "spiritual" in a materialistic and mechanistic society?

The traditional answers seem to offer us very little practical help. The disciplines of meditation, prayer, study of the Bible and so on are less and less regarded. The whole concept of silence, for example, is foreign to the age of the transistor radio.

But Brother Lawrence cuts right through these objections. What he is saying—if only we could see it in *our* setting—is timeless in its relevance. The man who could practice the presence of God in a kitchen has something worthwhile to say to the man who misses the presence of God in the accounting department. If he found a secret of serenity under pressure and tension (and he did), then we, *more* than our Christian predecessors, need to listen to him. He is the man for our times.

This book is, then, an attempt to re-interpret Brother Lawrence for twentieth-century readers. It is not simply a new translation, because if it were, all the problems of background and history would still separate him from us. Instead, I have taken the considerable liberty of transposing the Brother Lawrence of the past into the immediate present—from a monastery kitchen near Paris to a hospital kitchen in modern Boston. All the settings are changed; and the conversations become part of the endless search by contemporary Christians for a faith that is real and existential enough to survive and flourish in the unpromising soil of today.

So I have invented a new environment for "Lawrence Herman," and a new set of friends. But I have taken considerable pains to see that every opinion he expresses—every answer to a question—is substantially authentic "Brother Lawrence." Obviously the illustrations become modern ones (cars, planes, trade fairs), but the ideas are his, and can all be traced back to things he said that are recorded in his "Conversations."

Where the letters are concerned, there was less need to take liberties. Apart from giving his correspondents a modern setting, there was no need to do more than put his own forthright and burning love for God and for them into thoroughly modern language. Soldiers still get injured by accidents on active service. Men of sixty-four still worry that they are "finished." People in pain still wonder what possible purpose for God or man is achieved by their suffering. To each Brother Lawrence—alias Laurie, "the happy man"—has words of deep significance to say.

This man gave no glib answers. In that, at least, he seems incredibly "modern." He hated trivial devotion and half-hearted commitment. His letters are shining examples of honesty and integrity—even when he knew his words would hurt before they healed. He was a *great* man, and a great Christian. Without agreeing with every word he uttered, and without starting a new cult, modern Christians can expect to learn things from him that will revolutionize their lives.

1 UNDER THE CHESTNUT TREE

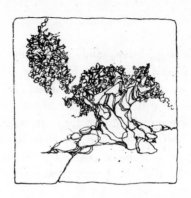

The first time I saw Laurie was the third of
August 1964, and the last time I saw him was
just three weeks ago. This book is all about
him—in fact, most of it is by him—but we had
to wait until he died before we could put it all
together. He hated publicity of any kind, and
if he had had his way no one would ever read
a word of what he had written, and nothing
would ever be reported of the things he said
and did.

But some of us—his friends and colleagues
at the hospital where he worked, and a few
others—felt that people had a right to know
about him. We believed that Laurie was
different in one vitally important way from
anybody we'd ever met. It's hard to pin it
down, or describe what he was like, without
sounding very "religious" and pious—and
Laurie was never like that.

The fact is, he lived his life—an ordinary,

hard-working, busy, and sometimes painful life—in God's company. Everyone who met Laurie, whether they were Christians, agnostics or even atheists, had to admit there was this "difference" about him. It wasn't just that he believed in God, or that he said his prayers, or that he witnessed to Jesus Christ (though he did all three). It was much more than that . . . he was in touch with God. He knew God. He lived in the presence of God every moment of every day. And if that sounds stupid, embarrassing or strange, then you never knew Laurie.

At any rate, some of us feel that Laurie had discovered something that changed the whole quality of living. The rest of us would worry, and rush around and get ulcers or take tranquilizers—and there he'd be, serene and smiling in the middle of it all, doing twice as much work as we did, without panic or complaint, and finding time to help those who were worried and spread the inner peace that was his own, personal trade mark. We tried to be Christians. We tried to pray. We tried to relate our faith to the changing, chaotic world around us, to our daily work, and to the problems of suffering, loneliness and fear. But Laurie seemed to do it without trying.

The Christian life—what the books call "the spiritual life"—seemed almost impossible for us in the modern world. Where could we be quiet? Where could we find tranquility? Where was God to be found in the jungle of machines and the throbbing clamor of the rush hour? Yet Laurie seemed to walk calmly through it all. He was unquestionably "spiritual"—but not because he had copped out of the modern world. He created his own little world of peace in the clatter of the hospital kitchen. He fashioned tranquility out of a half-hour lunch break in a locker room. He knew God, and talked with him, and seemed to live his whole day in his presence.

The result was that those who knew Laurie felt they knew God, too. Nobody else we have ever known had this remarkable effect on people—of drawing them closer to God, whoever they were.

So we decided to produce this memorial volume (again we can imagine what Laurie would have said about *that*!), because we believe that this ordinary man in an ordinary job had a quality of sanity and faith that usually eludes modern man; and that he had found an answer to the sort of problems that worry and distress many good Christians as well. He would never have written a book about it, simply because he never believed that what he had discovered was anything but the commonplace level of Christian experience. Probably it *should* be. Anyway, we hope that, just as knowing him and being his friends helped us to share his kind of life with God, so reading what Laurie said and did may help many others to find in all the excitement and confusion of the modern world the quiet inner peace that comes through living in the very presence of a God with whom there is "no variation or shadow due to change."

I first met Laurie when I went down to the Special Diets kitchen to check a delivery note for eggs. I was the food buyer for the hospital, and the S.D. kitchen was my biggest problem, with some patients needing extra protein, fat-free foods, or even particular kinds of fruit that had to be specially ordered through importers. I can't remember what the problem was with the eggs—probably the total on the order didn't tally with the total on the delivery note.

Well, there was this new man in the kitchen—new to me, anyhow. He was short and slightly bald, and wore round, cheap glasses. His white hospital coat was much too long for him, but it was spotlessly clean—a rare sight in our kitchens at that time.

But the first thing you noticed about Laurie was his smile. It wasn't big and hearty, and it wasn't a smirk or a grin. It had the sort of genuineness that makes you realize how seldom you see a real smile. It made you feel welcomed, relaxed, at home. At once you knew you were with someone who had a capacity for enjoyment, an inner contentment and a love of people. I know that sounds ridiculously exaggerated for an immediate reaction to one smile, but then—you never saw the smile!

He introduced himself as Laurie, and explained that he'd just been transferred to the S.D. kitchen. We quickly cleared up the egg mystery (whatever it was) and then as it was coffee-break time he poured me a cup and invited me to sit down and drink it with him.

"I think I've seen you at the Christian Fellowship a couple of times, haven't I?" he said.

I'd only been a couple of times and I couldn't remember having seen him there so I answered lamely, "Yes . . . I go when I can."

"You're a Christian, then?" The smile was hypnotizing me.

"I try to be," I replied.

"I don't," he said. "I gave up trying the day God taught me to trust him."

Now if anyone else had said that to me—the words were so confident, presumptuous, pious—I would have tuned him out right then. But Laurie could say it without offence and make it sound (as indeed it was) like a simple statement of fact. I found myself asking him when this had happened.

"When I was eighteen. It was strange,

really. I was out for a walk in the woods near Sudbury trying to think through some problems that had been on my mind for months. I'd been brought up to be a regular churchgoer, and for all my conscious life I'd believed in God and wanted to please him. I'd assumed that this was done by deliberate acts of worship, by prayer and study, by discipline and self-control—you know the sort of thing. And I was discouraged because, instead of getting better as I got older, I found I was actually getting worse. The harder I tried, the more I failed. I just couldn't see why God, who was supposed to be all-powerful, couldn't do a little miracle and fill me with instant goodness. Little miracle!—God forgive me!

"At any rate, I was walking along, thinking about these things, when I came to a very beautiful chestnut tree just north of the Post Road. I'd been watching it all year—the leaves coming fresh and green from the buds, the flowers opening up in early summer . . . and now it was loaded with chestnuts. The branches were quite weighed down with them.

"I sat under the tree—it's a lovely spot, near the Wayside Inn—and suddenly, like a ray of light bursting in my mind, I got the answer.

"It's hard to explain, but this is how it

came to me. In the winter, this old tree was bare, stripped of its leaves, apparently dead. With the spring the new life flowed up from the soil through its trunk and branches, reaching each branch and twig and pushing out the fresh leaves and the new growth. Then, later, the flowers and finally the fruit appeared, until on this still, sunny September day I could sit in its shade and see the wonderful crop of chestnuts on its branches.

"I was like the tree in winter. Myself, I was nothing—dead, barren, without fruit. And, like the tree, I couldn't change by struggling or sheer effort. I, too, must wait for the hand of my Maker to touch me with life, and change my winter of barren unfruitfulness—in his own time—into first the spring of new life and then the summer and fall of flower and fruit.

"Suddenly I saw what 'providence' was all about—it's simply believing that God has the power and the will to do all things well for us, if we will only submit to his loving, patient rule. And that nothing we can do—beyond trusting him—will speed up his will or make things happen which he isn't ready to do in us.

"At that moment, sitting there on the grass, my acts of worship, my attempts at discipline—all the effort I had put into trying to please God—were swallowed up in an enormous sense of love for him. The One who patiently led the trees and the plants through their seasons would also lead me, if I would only submit to his loving and powerful hand.

"I did. It was a real and true conversion, the result of the overwhelming sight of the majesty and love of God, of his providence and wisdom. I have learned more of his ways since then, and I know him better now and find greater joy in his company than I did on that day years ago. But I honestly cannot say that I love him any more now than at that moment, because there is a limit to the love humans can feel, and I believe at that instant I reached it in my love for a God so good, so patient, and so powerful."

We talked on—I wanted to know more about his conversion—until eleven-fifteen, which was the official, but customarily ignored, limit of the coffee break. At that point, Laurie put away the cups and went back to the carrots he had been shredding. As I left, he said he'd enjoyed our conversation and hoped we could talk together again.

2 ALL HE REALLY WANTS IS ME

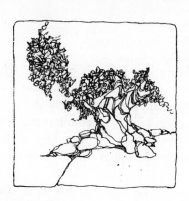

"Hi! May I join you?"

I looked up to see Laurie smiling at me, the steam from his soup giving his already cherubic face a quite disturbingly other-worldly glow.

"Why sure. Sit down."

"I thought the fried fish looked rather good." He began to spread his wares out on the table—soup (tomato), fried fish and chips, sweet roll, butterscotch pudding, and a cup of the cafeteria's own rather strong brew of coffee.

I was about to make my own little joke about deep fried coelocanth, when I checked myself. It wasn't that Laurie didn't enjoy a joke, but I remembered he always muttered a "grace" over his lunch, and somehow it seemed incongruous to ask a man to ridicule a fish for which he had just given thanks to God. You see—he was having an effect on me already.

Somebody had left a copy of the *Globe* on the table, and my eye caught the headline about a mass murder in Los Angeles.

"Grim, isn't it?" I commented, nodding towards the paper. "I just can't understand why people do such horrible things, can you?"

"Oh yes," he replied, his eyes suddenly catching mine, "I can. Honestly, nothing surprises me about the human race and its evils. It used to, I'll admit. It used to worry me a lot. I would ask myself how men and women made in the image of God could behave like this—and how God could allow it."

He sipped his soup slowly.

"But when I got around to thinking about it seriously, I realized what a mistake I had been making. After all, my conversion had awakened in me a great love for God—you remember, we were talking about it the other day in the kitchen—and the basis of that love was my amazement that someone as pure and holy as he is should offer love, and tenderness and forgiveness to a person as awkward, disobedient and failing as I am.

"Well, if I, in the light of all God's love and goodness to me, still find sinful thoughts and reactions a problem, what should I expect of people who have never known him? Quite frankly, far from being surprised at all the misery and evil in the world—things like this murder, here—I'm surprised there isn't more, considering how desperate man must be without God."

I toyed with my swiss steak and tried to put an elusive anxiety into words.

"Yes, I can see that, Laurie—in a way. I realize that man in rebellion against God is capable of very great evils . . . and I suppose it *is* rather stupid, really, to be surprised when we find people acting in exactly the way the Bible says they will. But—well, isn't there *anything* to be done about it? I mean, do we just wash our hands of it and say, 'There, look what a mess you're in without God. Serves you right!'?"

"No. No, not at all." Laurie spoke firmly. "That would be to imply that God has thrown up his hands and that the world is no longer his."

"Well, what do we do, then?"

"For myself," he said, his eyes glued to his food, (you couldn't take risks with the cafeteria cod), "I pray for those whose sins become public property—I mean, I *really* pray for them, as needing the love and mercy of God. And then I leave the whole thing to him, believing that God can and will, in his own good time, put right all the wrongs and injustices and sorrows of the world."

"And don't you feel bound to do what you can to put them right?"

"What I can, yes. But I realize that what *I* can do is so very little compared to the great need. That's no reason for not doing it, but it's a very good reason for believing that perfect justice, and perfect mercy, will one day come from God himself, and he will put right what we are helpless to deal with."

Writing down his words now, years after he spoke them, I'm aware of something that I was completely ignorant of at the time—that they could sound smug and unfeeling, as though he were saying, "Don't stew about human suffering and injustice; it'll all be all right someday."

All I can say is, that wasn't how it came to me across the small square table. Laurie's eyes were bright, alive with love, not hard with judgment, as he spoke. And when he said he *really* prayed for those whose sin hit the headlines, I knew that meant more than saying words about them: it meant that he would make their burdens his. I suppose you could say Laurie's views were those of a sensitive realist. He knew the heart of man, and he knew the heart of God.

Anyway, halfway through the dessert I asked Laurie how things were going in the hospital kitchen. I'd heard that they'd had two kitchen staff off sick and that things had been pretty hectic.

"Fine," he replied, without even stopping to think. "Fine. We're busy, you know . . . but it's a very satisfying job."

I was going to ask about the staff problems, when a shout made me look over towards the counter. I was just in time to see Selinda catch her elbow on a cart and drop a grossly overladen tray of plates, cups and cutlery. The explosion of metal and china was followed almost instantly by a great burst of laughter and applause. Selinda was very large and very clumsy—qualities which were considered to qualify her to be the butt of most of the hospital wits. In fact, one group of fellows and girls in a corner near the door began a chant of "B-u-t-t-e-r-f-i-n-g-e-r-s."

I turned back to say to Laurie how thoughtless it was of them to tease her. But he had left his seat, and was down on his knees near the counter picking up the broken pieces.

The noise died down, and eventually Laurie came back to finish the remains of his meal.

"Poor Selinda," he said, though his eyes were smiling. "They say lazy people take the most pains. Funny,"—a reminiscent chuckle—"that was a lesson I learned the hard way, too."

I looked interested, guessing some story from his past was coming up. It was.

"I used to work for a big banker—a Canadian, he was, head of their Boston office. He had a lovely Colonial home in Lexington . . . this was a while after my 'conversion,' remember? Well, my job was really to be a sort of assistant cook. I stood in for the chef on his days off, and the rest of the time I helped prepare vegetables, clean the kitchen and give a hand with general housework and odd jobs.

"The truth is I'm not all that good with my hands, especially when I'm nervous . . . which I often was in those days. And also I always wanted to get things done as quickly as possible.

"The result was that I soon had a reputation as a butter-fingers. Too many cups in the sink, too many plates on a tray and even—one horrible afternoon—too many antique vases on the table I was supposed to be polishing. I was told it had cost over five hundred dollars . . . when it was in one piece, you understand.

"The incredible thing was how kind everybody was about it. I found this more worrying than the actual breakages. No matter what I did my employer was always gentle and understanding, and so was the chef, for that matter. It began to upset me—that I should go unpunished when I was such a destructive menace around the house.

"In the end I couldn't stand it any longer—aren't we strange creatures? I believe I'd have stuck it out if they'd asked me to pay for the breakages out of my wages! But I decided I'd leave and go somewhere where my criminal carelessness would get its just rewards. For some obscure reason I felt both God and I would be satisfied if only I were made to suffer for my faults. So—believe it or not—I came here. I'd heard the work was hard, and the Food Service manager a real, old-fashioned disciplinarian.

"But what happened? Certainly nothing like I'd expected. From the day I arrived I've enjoyed every minute of it. Far from being a sort of punishment for my failures, every day I've spent here has been tremendously satisfying. No one had punished me, but God has given me a completely new understanding of himself.

"I suppose the whole thing is a picture of our inability to grasp what 'grace' really means—the completely undeserved favor of God. Like me in the banker's house, we find it harder to accept grace, tenderness and forgiveness than we do to accept punishment and pain. We want to *earn* God's approval . . . but even the best we can do would fall far short of that. God *gives* it to us, in the middle of our failures—if we put our trust in him, and love him, and give him first place.

"And that's the key. I used to spend a lot of time thinking up ways to please God—new acts of devotion, petty sacrifices of frivolities, longer periods of prayer and fasting. But now I've learned that all he really wants is *me*, and that these very 'things' that were meant to please him could be distractions from living all the time as though he were there.

"And he is. He's really there . . . not just 'in heaven', but right here in the cafeteria and down below in the Special Diets kitchen. If I've got him, what else could I possibly need?"

He glanced at his watch.

"Which reminds me," he said, grinning, "that when I get on my hobby horse I sometimes forget about the work I'm paid to do! I've *got* to go."

"Look," I said, "Laurie . . . I want to know more—about living near God, and all that."

"Fine," he said, stacking his plates carefully. "If that's what you really want, come see me again—some lunch-time? or evening?"

3   the Joys of the road

"Hello, Laurie. Welcome back."

He looked up, and the eyes lit up. Nice—how he always seemed genuinely glad to see you.

"Hi! Yes . . . and boy, am I glad to be back."

I couldn't resist a laugh.

"Give *me* four days in Miami Beach in exchange for this place and I wouldn't be glad to be back."

Laurie shook his head.

"I'm just not cut out for that sort of thing. Frankly, I wasn't looking forward to it."

"Tell me about it," I said, sitting down and nodding towards the electric clock over the kitchen door, which showed coffee time. He took the hint and put on the pot.

"Well, Ramsden was going, of course. It was an international display put on by manufacturers of diet foods—a sort of small-scale trade fair, I suppose. There's a lot of new stuff coming on the market—most of it for slimming, so far as I can see, but special protein foods and vitamin products—you can imagine the sort of thing.

"Well, as I say, Ramsden was going, but something came up and he asked me to go instead—keep my eyes open and bring home samples of stuff we might find useful. There were films and demonstrations, too—people were there from all over the nation, and Europe too.

"It was all a bit over my head. I'm not a qualified dietician. I'm a cook, let's face it. I've picked up a good deal but I'm not a businessman and I'm not an expert in any-thing. Still, as Ramsden couldn't go and somebody—apparently—had to represent the hospital, I couldn't refuse."

"But it went off all right?"

Again, the laugh.

"You *could* say so! The flight was pretty bad. You know I've got this weak ankle—well, it 'went' just as we were boarding, and every time the plane ran into turbulence it was agony. Still, it wasn't for long—and it stopped as soon as we landed.

"The display was fascinating and people were most helpful. I found that I was meeting the right people, without organizing it, and Ramsden was wild about the stuff I brought back."

"So you were worrying about nothing?"

"In a way. The truth is, I'd somehow managed to forget that going to a convention in Florida could be God's business just as much as working here in the kitchen—or leading a Bible study. I'd allowed the fact that it was an unwelcome job to blind me to the fact that God was calling me to do it.

"Anyway, a few days before I left I saw what was happening. I said to God, 'Lord, it's your work I'm doing, here in Boston, or down in Florida. I can't do even my daily work properly without your help, let alone these special jobs. Take away my uneasiness and give me a calm and trusting attitude, and help me to do my work to your glory here, there or anywhere.' "

"And he did?"

Laurie looked surprised at my question, "Of course. Have you ever known him to fail?"

The coffee was poured by now, and we still had ten minutes of our coffee break left. I mentioned something which Laurie had just touched on, and which had been on my mind for weeks.

"Laurie, your saying that makes me think of something else. Prayer."

His pale eyes crinkled at the corners, as though inviting me to proceed.

"You seem to find prayer so easy, Laurie—just like talking to"—I was going to say "someone you know," and realized that was exactly what it was, in his case—"talking to another human being. And God talks back to you. I don't find it easy at all . . . in fact, I have to *make* myself pray. How did you get into the way of turning so simply to God in prayer?"

"Human being!" Laurie smiled and repeated the phrase. "Another human being. Now if you'd said person, I'd have said that was the heart of it.

"God *is* a person. He's a personal God, not just a great creative Force. How else should we talk to him but as a person?

"Still, you asked how I got into the way of talking to him so simply, and that's a fair question. It wasn't always so simple, by any means.

"From the time when God became real to me, I knew that communicating with him—two-way communication—was the most important thing in the world. To communicate with everyone else and be deaf and dumb to God is to turn our priorities upside down, isn't it?

"Naturally, I don't mean communicating with him on a basis of equality, but on a basis of dependence. I had to talk with him, and he with me, because only he perfectly knows my

condition and circumstances and only he can
perfectly guide me through life. I knew that I
must learn to refer everything I did to
him . . . everything. That seems to me just
plain common-sense. An airline pilot keeps in
constant touch with ground control because
they know things he doesn't and can't know.
And that is why I keep in touch with God."

I said that I could see that, but though I
knew it was important, I still found it
difficult.

"At first I found it difficult, too. To say
it's important to talk with God and refer
everything to him isn't the same thing as
saying it's easy. To begin with, it requires
discipline and persistent effort. And I mean
that.

"Don't be fooled. Because I can talk with
God so easily and simply today doesn't mean
that it was always so. The price you have to
pay is willingness—willingness to control your
mind and thoughts, willingness to submit to
God's discipline, willingness to keep at it even
when you seem to make little progress.
Nothing worth having is easily achieved. Acts
of the will are the ones that matter most.

"But after a while—and I don't mean years
and years, but months or even weeks, if you
really mean business you will find that what
was hard effort has become a great joy.
Because you love God, and know he loves

you, the strain quickly goes out of the relationship, and his love excites you—that's the only word that really describes it—*excites* you with a longing to be with him and talk with him.

"You've seen people learning to drive a car? At first they have to concentrate on the techniques—you see their faces tight with concentration as they try to find the right gear, and so on. But as they master the technical side, and get plenty of practice, they stop 'driving' and start 'travelling'—until the time comes when driving is quite automatic and even subconscious, and they begin to appreciate the 'joys of the road'."

It was my turn to laugh, because Laurie wasn't a driver. But I got the point, and it was a good one.

"O.K. I can see that, Laurie. But how do you go about the 'techniques' of praying? Do you have set hours of prayer . . . what does Foster call it? A 'quiet time'?"

'Well—yes, I do have set times of prayer, and I believe they are a useful discipline, especially for a beginner . . . a learner, as you might say. But personally I don't worry much about them, and it wouldn't bother me if I were kept from keeping them at all. Put it this way: I don't *need* them. God is no nearer to me during my 'quiet time' than he is at this very moment in the kitchen; and prayer is no more real when it is said formally, on my knees by my bed, than when I say it informally over the sink or the oven. I really can't wait until ten at night or seven in the morning to refer some vital matter to God. I need him too much and too often to be able to leave things until a particular hour of the day. And his presence is so real that there is no danger that I'll forget to talk with him if I don't make an appointment with him!"

"So do you recommend me to have set times of prayer?"

"Yes—definitely. But not as an end in themselves, so that you say to yourself as you get off your knees in the morning, 'Well, that's my praying done for today.' That's just a bit of it—a concentrated dose, if you like. Set times of prayer are valuable in order to form a habit of conversation with God, and—as I said—referring all we do to him. They aren't the end itself, but means to an end. The end is God: being with him, living in his presence and under his control. You can't do that if you try to ration contact with God to twenty minutes twice a day or whatever it is."

Time was up. Laurie glanced at the clock.

"Look," he said, "We're just getting on to something very important. Why not come around to my room tonight and we'll pick up where we've stopped now?"

4 problems with prayer

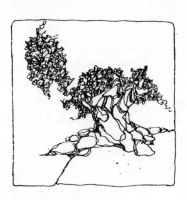

I didn't know the street existed, and it took me longer than I had expected to track it down, even though it wasn't more than half a mile from the hospital. Laurie had said "Come about eight" but it was a good deal later when I stood on the imposing front steps of a big old brownstone tenement and looked for the bell. I had always assumed he lived at the hospital.

The door was a double one, with dark glass windows, and everything seemed to be painted a dingy dark brown. Then I saw a small brass plate and by it an enormous, antique doorbell. The plate said "Brother-hood of St. Vincent", which startled me but I pushed the bell and waited. All seemed dark and silent inside.

After some minutes a light came on some-where along the entrance hall, and to my relief Laurie opened the door.

"I'm a bit late, I'm afraid . . ." I began.

"Oh, forget it! Everybody has a job finding us first time."

I went into the hall and he led the way up a wide, flight of stone stairs.

"Who's the 'us'?" I asked. "The Brotherhood of St. Vincent?"

"Yes. It's just a small Order—lay brothers, doing what the Rule calls 'practical works of mercy.' Vincent was a deacon, you see—ours is a serving Order."

He stopped at a plain door, painted the inevitable church hall brown again, and showed me into his room. It was small and very plainly furnished—an iron bed, a small table, two chairs and an old fashioned iron radiator . . . and a simple wooden cross on the wall above the fireplace.

"I didn't know you were a . . ."

"A monk?" he prompted, smiling. "I'm not. I'm just a lay Christian, like you, except that I've submitted myself to the Rule of this small Brotherhood. I do my ordinary day's work at the hospital, and live in the community here. There's nothing mystical or odd about it, I assure you."

He nodded towards one of the two chairs and I sat on it.

"I'll get a kettle on," he said, "We have a gas burner out in the corridor—primitive, but effective."

He left me alone for a minute or two while he saw to this, and I tried to adjust myself to this other picture of Laurie. It was all a bit . . . well, ecclesiastical. I'd never thought of him as anything quite so *churchy*.

Tea poured out, Laurie raised the subject we'd agreed to discuss—my problems with prayer. He suggested I start off by raising the difficulties I experienced—because, as he put it, "problems are very personal things, and so is prayer."

"Well," I said, "probably the worst thing of all is what one friend of mine used to call 'dry spells'—every now and again I hit a bad patch . . . it may last a month, or even longer . . . when I just can't get any *joy* out of praying. I feel as though it's just a routine, and my words aren't getting beyond the ceiling. Usually, I admit, I give up and don't pray at all until something or other starts me off again."

Laurie nodded. "Yes, I know the experience exactly."

"You mean—you've had it?"

He smiled. "Of course. I don't suppose a Christian exists who hasn't gone through what you've just described.

"Funnily enough, I think part of the answer is connected with the sort of thing that belonging to this Order involved. As I told you the other day, in general I don't rely too much on set times and patterns of prayer—I feel as near God . . . nearer, perhaps . . . in the hospital kitchen as in the chapel here, or kneeling by my bed. I think I said that when we first adopt the practice of prayer, set times are important to help us submit ourselves to God, but then they become less necessary as we learn to be with God and talk with him all the time—actually, they can even become distractions, at times.

"Much the same thing applies to these times of 'dryness'. For me, that's when the Rule becomes not a distraction but a prop for my faith—or lack of it. I believe God sends these 'dry spells'—I like your friend's phrase—to test our love for him. Does 'absence make the heart grow fonder'? Or is it a case of 'out of sight, out of mind'? If we can only love God when we feel he is near us then our love is immature and feeble. So God withdraws himself, sometimes, to test our love. And that is when our inner discipline—and these 'outer' disciplines of set times and patterns—should take over. Fidelity . . . faithfulness . . . is then the chief virtue."

"But it's hard, isn't it, Laurie? I mean, when the very act of being faithful seems irritating or unreal."

"Hard? Sure it is. There's an emotional, 'feeling' element in prayer and when that disappears, as it does in these dry times, then what was formerly a pleasure can be dull and may even feel 'unreal'. But love isn't *just* emotion. I mean, it's a relationship, isn't it? And whether I 'feel' it or not, I know God loves me and I know his will is best."

"O.K. I can see that keeping at it faithfully, even when God seems distant, is part of the answer. Do you just wait, then, for God to 'come back', as it were?"

Laurie smiled. "He isn't far from any of us . . . ever. But I see what you mean." He put down his empty cup, and thought for a moment. "Would you know what I meant if I said 'Make an act of resignation'?"

I shook my head.

"Well, it's jargon, I suppose. By an 'act of resignation' I mean a conscious and deliberate submission to the will of God."

"Say that again?"

"A point where you say to God, 'Lord, you are my God. You know what is best for me. You only can give me true joy. All my life lies in your hands. If this present dryness is because of my rebellion or wilfulness, or lack of faith, I here and now submit myself again totally to you, without any reserve, not claiming your presence as a right but resigning myself completely to your good and perfect will.' I have found—and so have others—that one such 'act of resignation', sincerely made, often not only ends the drought, but leads into new experiences of God."

I nodded, there not being much else to say, and raised another thing that had been bothering me.

"Right. But how do I make sure that I don't just simply 'forget' God? I must admit sometimes, at the end of a hectic day, perhaps, I've found myself in bed and suddenly realized I'd clean forgotten about praying. And often I go hours on end—days, I suppose, sometimes—without ever giving him a thought at all. That's terrible, isn't it?"

"I shall probably shock you," Laurie said, "but, honestly, no . . . it isn't terrible. Fortunately, God knows us better than we know ourselves. 'He remembers that we are only dust.' There's no point in getting all uptight about 'not thinking' of him. He's still there, whether I think about him or not. He doesn't change.

"When I find I haven't thought of God for a good while, I don't get depressed and guilty about it, but simply admit to him that I'm pretty forgetful (which I am), and then remind myself of his faithfulness and love.

"You may find this surprising—I mean, now that you know I'm part of this 'Order'— but I set very little importance indeed on all these penances and painful exercises that some people use to overcome their guilt at spiritual failures. Indeed"—he leant forward, as though sharing very significant—"I feel many sincere Christians don't get anywhere in the Christian life because they stick at penances and so-called 'exercises' instead of pressing on past them to the object of the whole thing, which is love of God. In the end, it makes them dry and self-centered, trying to fight their way back to God when he's right beside them all the time, waiting for them to turn to him and trust him. Faith . . . that's the key. Faith is the beginning and end of it all."

"I haven't got much faith," I said—and it came out more truly than I had intended.

Laurie lifted an eyebrow. "It's not a commodity, you know. Like coffee or toothpaste. It's more like a plant. It grows."

"I'm sure it grows for you, Laurie," I said. "But for me—well, I believe in God, and that's about it."

"Actually, that *is* it," Laurie cut in. "That's exactly it."

"When I first joined the Order—soon after my conversion—I found I was expected to spend several hours a day in prayer. The Prior gave me lots of advice and several little books of meditation, but I'm afraid I ignored the advice and left the books on my shelf. You see, that day in the woods I had met God . . . a God who was really there. I didn't see how exercises and forms could bring him any closer than he had been that day without them.

"So, I spent the hours appointed for private prayer in thinking of God."

It was my turn to lift an eyebrow, and Laurie noticed and smiled.

"All right, I know that sounds vague. But I didn't just kneel there and list his attributes, or recite acts of devotion to him. I set out first, to think through his divine existence— that he really and truly and objectively *exists,* as Someone quite other and apart from me, his creature. That was first, and I thought of him and all I knew of him from the Scriptures and in my experience until I was totally convinced that *God is.* I had no intention of spending my life in the presence of a Being who was simply a figment of my imagination.

"Then I spent hours letting that tremendous truth impress itself deeply on my heart—my feelings, if you like. Slowly, by letting my mind lead my heart, and by letting the light of faith shine into my feelings, I came to a point where my faith was alive and growing. I had absorbed, first, the knowledge, and then the love of God, and I resolved to do all I could to live from then on in a continual sense of his presence and, if possible, never to forget him again. There was no studied reasoning to prove the existence of God, and no elaborate meditation to inflame my devo-

tion to him. But I had been in his presence
—the living God—and I never wished to leave
it ever again."

5 The Purpose of Suffering

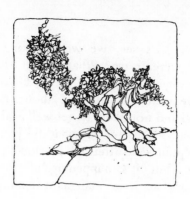

Robert looked as surprised as I had the first time I climbed the stairs to Laurie's room. Every footstep squeaked alarmingly and echoed between the bare stone walls, and the unrelieved expanses of dark brown paint.

"Well, you told me it would be a shock, but I didn't quite associate old Laurie with this sort of place."

I laughed, and led the way on to a small landing. Laurie must have heard us coming, for the door opened before I could knock, and the darkness was suddenly split with light from his room. Robert followed me in, his eyes taking in the simple furnishings and religious objects, and then Laurie was fussing around making coffee and soon we were both oblivious to the surroundings. When we were all comfortably sipping our hot coffee, Laurie raised again the subject we'd asked him about in the canteen that very day.

"Now, let's see, we were talking about Marion, weren't we? What was it that was bothering you, Robert—I mean, beyond the thing we were all saddened about, that she was so ill and not likely to get well again?"

"It was this matter of—what did you call it, John?—'pointless suffering'. Marion's just one example, but it's happening all the time. It's . . . it's as if a malignant enemy were following us, waiting to pounce out of the shadows and ruin our lives. Surely that can't be God's will?"

Laurie thought for a moment, gazing at his steaming cup in silence.

"Why do you say 'pointless', Robert? How do you know Marion's suffering is 'pointless'?"

"Well, it's hard to see . . ."

"Of course it's hard to see. We've got such a limited perspective—a sort of 'worm's-eye view' of life. It might look quite different from God's viewpoint. It might even look quite different from Marion's, especially when it's all over."

"That's fair enough, Laurie," I chipped in. "But surely that's rather cold comfort to Marion? I mean—as she actually goes through all the searing pain . . . it must be hard to keep telling yourself, 'There's some point in this, somewhere.' "

Robert leaned forward, and tossed in the

question we'd both been avoiding—not just
that night, but every time we'd talked with
Laurie on the subject of pain.

"Look, Laurie," he said, "Forgive me
putting it like this, but there's no point in
beating about the bush. You're very stoical
and fatalistic about suffering, in theory. But
how would you react if it were happening to
you?"

"Not fatalistic." Laurie got that in quickly.
"That's pagan. Not even stoical, really, because I'm not at all brave or courageous.
More—how can I put it?—*trusting* . . . trusting
that my all-knowing God knows best.

"To be frank, I *do* expect that one day,
perhaps quite soon, I shall experience some
great pain of body or mind. As a matter of
fact, my health has never been all that great,
and at any age I must be prepared for some
illness and pain.

"But the way I look at it is this: I ask
myself what could be the worst thing that
could possibly happen to me. The answer is
crystal clear—it would be to lose this sense of
God's presence, which I have enjoyed for
many years. That would be the ultimate
disaster and the bitterest pain—and my mind
recoils in horror from the thought of it. But
God has assured me, in his own written
promises, and in the assurance he has given
me in my own heart, that he will 'never leave

me nor forsake me'.

"That means that, whatever else, the worst imaginable thing *simply cannot ever happen to me,* and compared with that no pain of body or mind has any real power over me. After all, the greatest pains—or the greatest pleasures—of this world can't be compared with what I have already experienced of both kinds in the spiritual state. Once I am sure that God will deliver me from all spiritual evils, through the blood of Jesus Christ, I find that physical evils are rather cut down to size—seen in their true perspective."

"Do you mean," I asked, "that you would simply grin and bear them?"

Laurie permitted himself one of his wonderful, understanding smiles.

"No, of course not. What I mean is that if God has perfectly provided for the greater evil—spiritual pain and loss—I am completely confident that he can and will take care of the lesser evil of physical pain. I believe that he would give me strength to bear whatever evil he permitted to happen to me, and so I don't need to worry about that."

"But that still doesn't answer the charge that such suffering is pointless." Robert was sticking to his case.

"Well—nothing is pointless for the Christian, is it? But sometimes we have to search pretty hard to find what its point is.

"Look—when we set out on the Christian life, our two basic needs are to know Christ and to know ourselves. The interesting thing is, that as we get to know him better, we get to know ourselves better, too—and we find how unworthy we are—of the name of 'Christian'. Like the apostle Paul, we judge ourselves the 'foremost of sinners'. We come to see that our fallen natures, so easily drawn to every kind of sin, are responsible for most of the troubles and sorrows of life, both in us and in our circumstances. And we have to admit that whatever pain comes to us is less than we deserve, and to submit ourselves to it, and bear it as long as God calls us to do so, will bring its own spiritual advantages and blessings . . . now, or later. Perfect resignation to God's will—that is, trusting acceptance of it—is the sure way to heaven, and light from heaven floods the path.

"I'm sorry," he added, the smile breaking through again. "That sounded like a sermon."

"And a rather negative one, at that," said Robert (but he was smiling, too). "I can see that there may well be blessing in this kind of fortitude and—what did you call it?—trusting acceptance. But aren't there more positive elements in the Christian life?"

"Yes," I said, before Laurie could reply, "I've often wanted to ask you that. What do we *do*—I mean, actively—to become better

Christians . . . What are the basic requirements?"

"You're asking for another sermon!"

"No, just your own experience, Laurie . . . It's a question we often raise at our fellowship meetings, but everybody gives different answers."

"Well, St. Paul said that there are three things that last forever: faith, hope and love. My experience is that those three are the permanent elements of any man's relationship with God."

"Uh, could you repeat that?" Robert had obviously got lost somewhere in that last sentence.

"Faith, hope and love are what it's all about," Laurie paraphrased. "Through faith we believe his promises and have hope. Through faith and hope we come to love him, and for love of him we want to please him in everything we do. So faith, hope and love combined unite us to the will of God. We believe in him, and so we go where he leads. He is our only hope, and so we cling to him whatever comes. And we love him, and so set out to please him by what we think, what we say, what we do.

"Somebody has put it this way: All things are possible to him who believes; they are less difficult to him who hopes; they are not difficult at all to him who loves; and they are easy to him who keeps on doing all three."

Robert was shaking his head.

"It all sounds so impressive," he said staring at his toes, "And I'm sure you're right. Sitting here I can believe it all, and I honestly think that if I were in a different sort of job—living in a community like this, perhaps, or farming peacefully somewhere, or working as a missionary—I could succeed as a Christian. But how can you think in terms of faith, hope and love when you spend your working life ankle deep in electronic equipment, always ten minutes behind schedule and besieged by people who want their machines back yesterday. I can hardly get around to thinking of lunch, let alone thinking of God—and everything I do is so totally *secular*."

Laurie laughed.

"Sounds just like the S.D. kitchen to me. But what makes you think that God is absent from the maintenance shop but present in the chapel? Where's your doctrine of God? In any case, holiness doesn't depend on changing our jobs, *but in doing for God's sake what we have been used to doing for our own.*

"Seriously—repair the equipment for God, answer the abusive phone calls for God, concentrate fully on the job you're doing for God. He isn't obsessed with *religion*—he's the God of the whole of life. But we need to give it to him, consciously turning it over into his hands. Then whatever we're doing—provided it is not against his will—becomes an act of Christian service.

"In fact, I'd go so far as to say that the very best way of coming closer to God that I have yet discovered—far better than those dreary mechanical 'devotions' recommended by some of the text-books—is to do my ordinary, everyday business without any view of pleasing men, but as far as I can, purely for the love of God. That was what St. Paul was talking about . . . let me see, where is it?"—he laboriously extracted his Bible from the plain bookcase near his bed—"In Galatians, I think. Yes, here it is: 'Am I now seeking the favor of men, or of God? Or am I trying to please men? If I were still pleasing men, I should not be a servant of Christ.' "

We sat for a moment silent, because there didn't seem to be much more to say. That left Laurie the last word.

"Honestly, I feel closer to God in the kitchen than I usually do during a chapel service."

6 ALL FOR THE ALL

Dear Fiona,

To be honest, I find your request a very difficult one. On one hand, I long to see you grow in the Christian life, having had a small part in planting the seed of faith in your heart. On the other hand, the experience God has given me is so precious, and so private, that I have always been reluctant to speak of it, or let it be known how he has come to me. Spiritual pride is an ugly and dangerous thing, and too often I feel it at my shoulder.

But how can I refuse you? It is natural, and right, that you should want to feel God's continuing presence. It is part of your birthright as a child of God. And I know you are sincere in this, if only from the number of letters you have written and your determination to wring from me somehow the method (as you call it) by which I found this great blessing from God.

So I am going to tell you—but on one condition. You must not show this letter to anybody else. If I thought for one moment that you would let it be seen, all my longing for your growth in Christ could not persuade me to put these words on paper. However, assuming—as I must—that you will respect my confidence, here is my story.

After my conversion (which you know about) many people pressed various spiritual books and manuals on me, all offering different, and sometimes conflicting, advice about the Christian life, personal devotions, prayer, and so on. Faced with all these different ways of going to God, I decided to wash my hands of them all. They only served (it seemed to me) to confuse what must surely be an essentially simple thing. All I wanted to know was: how could I put myself completely in God's hands?

This led me to a phrase which kept coming back into my mind: *to give all for the All.* As a concept it seemed so much more clear-cut than the exhortations in the text books. He would give—indeed, *has already given*—all, and it is blasphemy to offer less than all to him. There and then I laid myself before God, and renounced, for love of him, everything that was not of God, and began from that moment to live as if there were no one in the whole world but he and I.

Sometimes I saw myself, where God was concerned, as a criminal in court, looking up at the judge. At other times I saw myself as his favored son, looking up into the eyes of my loving Father. As often as I could I expressed my thanks and worship to him, and I consciously kept my mind in his presence, and called it back whenever it wandered off after other things.

This wasn't easy, of course, but I kept at it. Let me make one thing clear—my attitude was not a product of abject fear, nor of rigid discipline. It was the product of love. When my mind wandered, or got distracted with "worldly" things, I didn't go in for an orgy of remorse, but quietly turned my thoughts back to him. And I practiced this all the time— thinking of God, reminding myself of his goodness, love and holiness, even in the middle of preparing a high-protein breakfast or dealing with complaints from patients. It's not as difficult as it sounds, once you get away from the idea that there are set times to pray and set times *not* to pray!

Well, that's the way it's been all these years. And imperfect though it has been, the most tremendous blessings have flowed into my life from it. I well realize—I emphasize it to you, Fiona—that these blessings are simply, solely and entirely of the mercy and goodness of God. No "method" or "technique"—

whether mine, or those in the books I mentioned—can *do* any of it without him. And no one can *be* anything without him—I less than any.

But my experience is that when we are faithful to keep ourselves in his presence, and keep him constantly "before our eyes," it keeps us from willfully offending him, and so preventing his grace and power from flowing into our lives.

But more than that: to live with God always beside us creates in our hearts a holy freedom and—if I may put it in such words—more familiarity with God than all the devotional aids on earth. We are not meant to be cramped, tongue-tied, fearful or hesitant in his presence. The Son has come to "set us free." What happens, I believe, is that by continually remembering him our sense of the presence of God becomes at first *habitual,* and then delightfully *natural.* That is my "method," if one may use such a word about a practice which is now as normal to me as breathing.

Please don't write to thank me for this letter. Give God thanks, if you wish, for his great goodness to me, which I can never deserve.

May you, and I, and all things praise *him.*

Yours in the Lord,
LAURIE

7 The Touches of God

My dear Bishop,

Forgive me for bothering you with this letter, but you've always helped me so much in the past that I felt you were the right person to turn to for advice, or your opinion, on a subject that disturbs me a good deal.

You know, from some of our past conversations, of the way in which God has blessed me for many years. You were kind enough to say once that if all your clergy and workers enjoyed a similar walk with God most of our problems in Christ would disappear overnight. But you also know of the opinions of some of those I love and respect most, including some in the Brotherhood, who feel otherwise about God's dealings with me, and it is on this that I should be glad to have your thoughts. I have searched through books for the story of a similar experience to mine—to prove that it is not so extreme or peculiar—but have failed to find anything quite like it.

A few days ago a deeply spiritual person took me to one side and told me that the Christian life was a life of grace which began with abject fear of God, grew with the hope of eternal life and was perfected in a pure love for him—and that we all must go through these three stages.

Now, sir, this is my dilemma; If what he said is true, and exclusively so, then my belief is not true Christian faith at all, and my daily experiences of God are not real, but fantasies. But I *know* it is authentic and that they are the genuine touches of God on my life.

For me, these stages of fear, hope and love have little positive meaning. In fact, they are actually discouraging. That is why, from the day I joined the Brotherhood, I have set myself simply and solely to know and love God *himself,* and to renounce all substitutes and formulas—even religious ones.

I must admit that for about ten years after that, I suffered a great deal, spiritually. Having resolved, like many Christians before me, to meditate frequently on death, judgment, heaven, hell and similar serious themes, I found that it was my sins that were also in front of my eyes, and my great failure. At times it seemed that events, reason, and even God himself, were against me, and only *faith* stood on my side. But the effect of this was to make me cling to God, at the thought of the great and undeserved kindness he had shown one as sinful and full of failure as I was. And from that came what I can only call a tremendous *appreciation* for God (respect is too weak, reverence too cold—there really isn't a word for it), which itself produced from time to time a sense of great delight and consolation in him.

At that point I was sometimes troubled, I must admit, by the thought that to believe I had received such favors was a colossal presumption—pretending to be at one leap where other and better men only arrived after a life-time of difficulty. I sometimes even wondered whether it was not a willful delusion, a trick of Satan, and that in truth I was lost.

But eventually, as you know, after some ten years of this tension between great joy and great anxiety, God gave me a profound inward peace, as though my soul had finally arrived at her center and place of rest. I did not *believe* any more than before, but the sense of unrest and conflict was taken away and—thank God—has never returned. And from that day I have tried to walk before God very simply, in faith, in humility and in love for him, trusting that when I have done what I can, he will do with me what he pleases. I would not take up a piece of paper from the floor against his orders, nor from any motive but from my love of him.

I have, as you know, given up all set forms of devotion and prayers (except those which the rule of the Order obliges me to fulfill). I just always enjoy an habitual silent and secret conversation of the spirit with God—and sometimes, I am afraid, this inward joy or rapture is so intense that I have to strongly control myself to keep from disturbing or embarrassing people around me.

Why I am writing to you, sir, is this. Some good men, as I have said, now tell me that I have got it all wrong. They say that it is a delusion, that it is pietistic, too "other-worldly", to remote from the world and its problems, too self-centered.

And I cannot bear that this inexpressible joy, this union with God, should be called delusion. I want nothing but God. If this is delusion on my part, surely God would show me, and put it right? He would not leave me for so long in self-deception. Let him do as he wishes with me. Is that "other-worldly"? I want only him. Is that to be "self-centered"?

But I do not want to defend my own experience of God. Indeed, I do not need to, for he is judge. But, as I have always respected your opinion, and as some of my Christian friends are clearly worried about me, I should be grateful if you would tell me whether what God has done with me is so very exceptional, or so remarkably extreme. Or is it, as I suspect, so very normal that men are afraid of it, and miss, through fear, the love that casts it out?

Yours very sincerely in the Lord,
LAURIE

8 he's near, and you'll know it

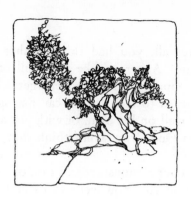

Sgt. J. F. Conway
FR228624131
Signal Corps Det 63
A.P.O. New York 09324

Dear John,
How good to hear from you! Naturally we had been wondering how you were getting on—we had heard a little news from Ralph, and we pray for you from time to time at our Fellowship meetings, but it was a great joy for me to hear from you directly, and to find that your main concern now, as it was when you were with us at the hospital, is to know and love and serve God better.

Now—about the matter you raised.

First of all, let me say I wasn't surprised to hear that you had run into difficulties. I must admit I had always expected that some day God would put you to the test in this sort of

way. After all, you had things rather easy,
hadn't you! A person like you—full of personality, popular, active and energetic—is always tempted to feel that he can manage life
perfectly well on his own, or with just a little
help from God. You won't think that again,
will you?

About your circumstances. I can, of course,
give little advice. You were so eager to join
the Army (and I am not blaming you for that,
or saying it was a wrong decision)—and to see
the world. I realize that a small military base
in a hostile sheikdom, with nothing but
burning sand in every direction, no proper
leave for six months and very little relief from
the incessant heat, is not exactly what you
expected: but it's what you've got, and
whatever you've got has come by God's
permission, and is at this moment his will for
you. Believe that!

But I gather from your letter that it's not
simply the circumstances that have got you
down. You rightly see that the true issue is
within yourself, and I must say I am glad—
yes, *glad*—that this is so. You say God doesn't
"come to you" any more. He will, in his own
good time, and when you least expect it.
More to the point is, do you "come to God"?
From your letter, I believe that you do, and
this is why I am glad about what is happening
to you. You have not let your depression

bury your concern for God. Probably for the first time in your life, you are facing really man-sized difficulties—but that is bringing to the surface a man-sized faith. And that's cause for rejoicing!

So, John—hope in God more than ever. Thank him—as I do now—for the favors he is doing you, especially for the patience and determination he has given you during this difficult and testing time. That in itself is the best possible proof of the care he takes of you. Let that encourage you, and be sure to thank him for it.

I can see how Michael's accident has depressed you. It must have been wonderful to meet him out there after all that time—and what a strange meeting place! I read about the incident, of course, in the papers, but had no idea another former member of our Fellowship was one of those injured by the mine.

As you say, the injury itself (thank God) was not too serious. More serious is the way it has affected both Michael's faith, and yours.

I have always felt—and have told him to his face, in the past—that Michael should really put his mind to growing up as a Christian. His heart is in the right place, his character is excellent, but sometimes he seems to be rather immature in his attitude to things, and a little caught up in "the world". I know it's hard for healthy, lively young men like you two to apply your minds to subjects like death, judgment and heaven—but there is no way to Christian maturity without it, believe me.

So even this accident, you see, can have a good result, because it can compel you both to turn your minds to serious and important matters. Michael, certainly, will have plenty of time in the hospital to do some real thinking—do urge him, won't you, to see how what has happened to him underlines his need of God? He may feel it proves God has deserted him. But that kind of thinking makes God little more than a good luck mascot. In fact, an accident like this should drive a spiritual man to renew his total trust in God, who goes with him everywhere, and keeps him in joy and pain, in pleasure and sorrow, in life *and in death.*

Turn it all to prayer and faith. That's my advice in a nut-shell. Think of God as often as you can, and especially in times of danger. Just a little lifting up of the heart is enough—a little remembrance of God, a brief act of inward worship—even out on patrol, or on guard with a rifle in your hands: God hears and understands. He is near, and you will know it.

Don't think this in any way lessens your ability or efficiency as a soldier. Far from it. The man whose courage is built only on his own resources can never match the man who is drawing on the courage of Christ.

So here is my advice to you both. Think of God as often as you can. Cultivate the habit, by degrees, of turning consciously to him at every opportunity, no matter how briefly. Make these small, holy acts of worship and prayer. No one need see or know (none of those barrack-room bedside dramatics—prayer is not for public performance), and what I am suggesting is not very difficult. All it requires is the will to do it. And it seems to me absolutely necessary for men in your position, whose lives and whose spiritual standing are under constant attack, to know where to turn for help at any moment.

God bless you both. You know I am praying for you, and I trust you pray for all your former colleagues and brothers in Christ here, and for me.

Yours,
LAURIE

9   A LOW PLACE FOR GRACE TO FLOW

Dear Richard,

Yes, you are right. There *is* a brother in our Society who has had—and, in fact, daily enjoys—just the experience you describe. I do know him, and am delighted to tell you a bit about him. Then perhaps, if you are still interested, you may care to meet him and decide whether what I am about to tell you is truth or exaggeration. Anyway, I'm grateful for the opportunity to write to you about him, because I believe simply recounting what God has done in him and with him will be a blessing to both of us: me in the telling, and you in the reading.

The man you describe has been seeking a deeper knowledge of God for more than forty years. I don't think it would be an overstatement to say that throughout that time—since his conversion as a young man—his chief ambition has been to think, say and do nothing that would displease God. Of course, he has often failed (and is the first to admit it), but this man has such a heightened sense of gratitude to God that he longs to show his love for him by pleasing him in everything.

For about the last thirty years this longing to please God has given him an amazing sense of God's presence with him all the time. Probably because of this deep desire to show his love for God, he has had a greater awareness than the rest of us of the fact that *God is there.* You may say, "Well, of course God's there." But how real is that to you? Is it much more than an article of the faith? For this brother—who, I must stress, claims to be no better than the rest of us, just more blessed—it is the most important and influential fact of existence. He is, quite simply, always with God. And this presence gives him such joy that at times he has to take steps to prevent his inward ecstasy from spilling over and embarrassing others.

It is true that his actual experience of God's presence varies in its intensity. Sometimes, usually when he is very busy at his daily work (he's a cook in a hospital kitchen), there are occasions when he becomes aware of the divine *absence*—not that God has gone away, but that he has forgotten that he is there, rather like a familiar friend or loved one who is sitting in the room with you while you are concentrating on something else.

What happens then, as he describes it, is that God "makes himself felt". As this happens—as though God were nudging him—he either silently lifts his heart to God in love and praise or, when circumstances make it possible without embarrassing other people, he actually puts it into words. One of his prayers on these occasions, he tells me, goes like this:

> O my God,
> Here I am.
> All that I am is yours.
> Make of me whatever you want.

Then it seems to him as if God, contented even with these few words, settles down again in the depth and center of his being.

Now I know that's a strange way to put it, but it is how he describes the experience, and I can confirm that in everyday life he certainly retains a vivid sense of God's nearness. So much so that he is now incapable of doubting the reality of it.

One obvious result of this (obvious to those of us who know him, that is) is this brother's air of total peace and contentment. Unlike the rest of us, he is not endlessly and restlessly searching for God, but has all the richness of God constantly available to him and enjoys him constantly.

I remember this brother giving an address

in chapel one evening. Usually he is reluctant to talk about his experiences, but on this occasion he seemed so full of God he had to speak. He rebuked us—very gently and loving-ly, let me add—for our blindness to the true riches that were within our grasp. He felt sorry for us (he said), who were like million-aires living on the old age pension. "God has got so much to give," he said, "and yet we are content to pick up spiritual trifles. Our blindness and disobedience hinder him from working in our lives. They are like a dam built across a flowing stream, stopping its course and cutting off the life-giving supplies of water to the thirsty ground below.

"But when God finds a heart that is ready, open and trusting, the obstacle is swept aside, and the pent-up waters flow as never before, surging into every corner and hidden place, bringing light and joy.

"We stop the current," he warned us, "mainly by the way we undervalue God's gifts. Simply to want him, above anything else, is the way to set the waters of life flowing.

"So—let us hold him back no longer. Let's break the dam that stops his blessings. Let's make a way for grace to flow, making up for the wasted, arid years of spiritual drought by clearing the gulleys and the gutters and letting the stream burst through.

"Let's enter into ourselves and root out all that holds back the river of God. We must keep at it, because not to advance, in the spiritual life, is to go back."

It was a moving talk and I have passed it on to you hoping that you will do what we all did that night—compare his experience of God with your own, and let his words and example melt away any coolness of heart or failure of faith you may have experienced. I think our brother would want me to add that it is not at all a question of doing what he has done (as though he had achieved this state by his own efforts or merit), but of receiving, by faith, what he has received. The river flows wherever there is low land cleared ready before it. The thirsty land does nothing but drink up the goodness.

So let us both profit from this man's experience of God. He is not at all well-known, outside these four walls and the hospital kitchen, but he is known to God, as we are. Believe me, Richard I have *personal knowledge* of all this—you may well have guessed already what I mean by that.

Yours in the Lord,
LAURIE

10 EMPTY-TO BE FILLED

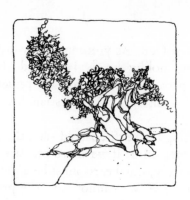

Dear Andrew,

I received two books and a letter this morning from Joan—you remember her? She helped us with our children's club a few years ago, when we were working in Springfield. Since then she has spent two years in a convent, and now she is preparing to make her profession as a nun. She particularly asked me to request your prayers for her, and also the prayers of your fellowship.

I feel she needs our prayers. It's a big step she is taking. We must pray that the motive for her renunciation of the world is the only right one, love of God alone, and that she is willing to devote herself wholly to him.

I was interested in the books she enclosed, and am sending one of them on to you. It deals with a subject which, in my opinion, sums up the whole business of living the spiritual life in the workaday world—the presence of God. As you must know by now, this is my hobby horse! I really do believe that the person who practices the presence of God will soon find his Christian life transformed.

One thing I have discovered—and this book, too, touches on it: if we are to practice God's presence truly, our hearts must be emptied of everything else. We cannot have the presence of God *and* an ambition for fame or money. We cannot have the presence of God *and* a love of luxury, or success, or prestige. I am not saying that only those without talents or without money can achieve the presence of God. I am saying that our desire must be first and foremost for him, with these other things taking the places he has allowed them to have in our lives. He cannot possess our hearts unless first he has emptied out the part that is already filled by someone or something else. And he cannot get to work in our hearts and do whatever he pleases there, until he is given all the room to work in.

But this is not a dry, negative, hard thing. It is not the end of pleasure, but its true beginning. For there is no life more delightful or satisfying than one spent in continual conversation with God, as anyone who has experienced it will testify. But let me add a warning: don't set out to practice the presence of God *in order to* obtain these joys and pleasures. It is God we seek, not delights or satisfactions. We long to be with him because we love him, not because he hands out good things to those who are nearest to him.

Sometimes I feel, Andrew, that if God had called me to be a preacher, I should preach on this subject every time I entered the pulpit. And if I were a spiritual counsellor, I should urge everyone who came to see me to seek God instead. That's how important I believe it to be—and it is all so *simple,* too!

If we could glimpse for one moment the enormous need we have of God's grace and help, we should be unwilling to lose contact with him even for one second. We can't draw a single breath or lift a finger without him, much less fight spiritual battles and overcome the cunning and malice of the Evil One. It is high time we all resolved never willfully to forget him, and to spend the rest of our days in his presence. If we did, we should soon see the difference—in our own lives, and in our churches.

> Pray for me, as I do for you.
> Yours in Christ,
> LAURIE

II   THE DANGER OF "KEEPING THE RULES"

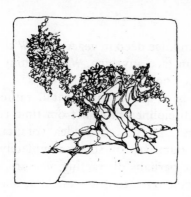

Dear Tom,
Thanks for sending back those few articles—
Mrs. Davies brought them in yesterday.

However, I was a bit surprised that you
haven't yet made time to give me your
thoughts on the little book I sent you a
month ago. Did you receive it? I'm rather
worried that you should ignore it, not because
I sent it (after all, it's hardly the first book
we've lent each other, is it?) but because the
subject is terribly important. *Please*, Tom—
read it, and start putting it into practice now,
old as you are. Better late than never, as they
say.

For myself, I simply do not understand
how devout Christians like yourself can be
satisfied with a religion that does not give
them day by day the presence of God. After
all, what else is there? In the depth of my
being I keep myself shut away with him, even

when I'm knee deep in vegetables! With him, I feel I can face anything. Without him, everything becomes unbearable.

This is a matter of mental, rather than bodily discipline: though from time to time, of course, it is a good idea voluntarily to deprive ourselves of some completely innocent but perhaps distracting pleasure, simply to sharpen our attention on him, and show him that we are serious when we say we want him above everything else.

I don't mean by that that we should physically ill-treat ourselves, or go in for the sort of proud self-denial which St. Paul scorned.[1] God's service is perfect freedom. We have to do our work, whatever it is, faithfully, without letting it dominate us or disturb our inward peace of mind. That in itself is a mental discipline, not spectacular, but demanding: to serve man, as God commands, and to keep in contact with him while we are doing it.

I know that you, Tom, are a great one for a "disciplined devotional life". You like to have rules, and keep them. But surely the danger is that the rules, and even the devotions, may cease to be means to an end—knowing God— and become an end *in themselves*. When, through practicing his presence, we are with God, who is our end, it is rather pointless to return to the means again. We can stay in his presence by expressing our love in any way which our spirits suggest—by prayer, by acts of thanksgiving, by doing our work to his glory, or by abstaining from some distracting luxury for a time. But by then we shall be in no danger at all of confusing the end with the means. We shall be in no danger of worshipping our own devotions!

Tom—I know you well enough (and you know me) to be able to say this. Time is running out. Persevere in seeking God, and his daily presence . . . and keep at it until your dying day. Pray for me, as I shall for you.

Yours in the Lord,
LAURIE

[1] Colossians 2:20-23.

12 he wants so little; he gives so much

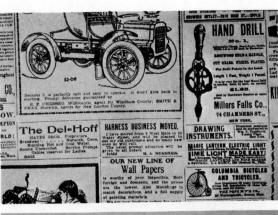

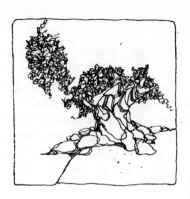

My dear Gordon,

I was very touched by your letter, and can only say, I know how you feel. I didn't realize you were past your three-score years, but I can well remember the particular heart-searchings I went through at about your time of life and so I can sympathize. But there is nothing so very special about being sixty-four, like you—or seventy-nine, like me! What are years in a calendar to our God, with whom a thousand of them are only one day?

I feel you should set out to make the most of your retirement, not see it as the stage before the grave. Look at it this way: someone else will have to worry now about your business, and you are free, with time as never before, to enjoy drawing near to God. Until now the daily pressure of earning your living has made it difficult for you to have time—unhurried time—for him. Now that will be a problem no longer, granted the will on your part to do it.

And it isn't hard work! He requires so little, and gives us so much: a little remembering of him from time to time; a little lifting up of the heart in praise; a brief offering to him of the joys or sorrows of the moment—and he is there. Turn to him, Gordon, all the time—when you are with friends, when you are enjoying your meal: brief though your recognition of him is, he will accept it, and he will come. He is so much nearer to us than we realize.

This doesn't mean you've got to spend your life in church, either! We can make sanctuaries of our hearts and draw aside from time to time within their quiet walls to talk with him. I believe that everyone—yes, *everyone*—is capable of this close, familiar relationship with God, though perhaps not all equally . . . but that doesn't matter, because he knows our capabilities. The important thing is to make a start at it. He may be waiting for you to make *one* real and costly decision to turn to him, and then it will all be easy.

Don't lose heart. We are both no longer young. Let's be determined to live and die with him. Nothing else really matters. Don't get caught up in scrupulous observance of devotional rules or forms, but act as though

you had confidence in God, as I know you
have. Pray for me, as I do for you.

In Christ,
LAURIE

13 GRASSHOPPER MINDS

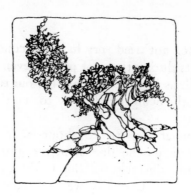

My dear Robert,

I'm so glad you wrote to me about your problem of wandering thoughts in prayer. It is much more common than you think, but many devout Christians are quite unwilling to admit to it, in case it should appear that they were not as whole-heartedly devoted to God as they wish to appear.

The truth is, we all have grass-hopper minds. We leap from thought to thought all the time. It is the hardest thing in the world to control our thoughts. But the will is still the master of our faculties, surely? Nothing can happen in our minds that is contrary to our wills. So the will must trap and subdue our thoughts, and carry them finally to the feet of Christ.

Mind you, once the bad habit of wandering thoughts has got a foot-hold, it is not easily dislodged. If over a long period our will has failed (or not tried very hard) to control our thoughts during times of prayer, even against our will, as it were, we may find our thoughts constantly being lured away to the things of the earth.

So, what can we do about it? You have already taken the first step: recognizing the need, and sincerely wanting to do something to correct it. Certainly we shall confess this fault to God, and humble ourselves before him, aware that to treat him casually is the final blasphemy against our Creator and Lord.

But is there any positive, practical advice I can give?

Well, I can offer one piece of negative advice! Don't pray long, wordy prayers. The longer and more wordy the prayer, the more likely our mind is to wander away from it. The same thing happens, after all, in a long and tedious conversation. God looks for quality, for intensity, rather than duration. It's not how long we pray that matters, but how sincerely and fervently. A rambling discourse on our knees is a certain recipe for wandering thoughts in our heads.

Instead, take the position in prayer before God of a dumb or helpless beggar at a rich man's gate. It is the beggar's responsibility to be alert to the rich man's moves. In the same way, make your times of prayer times of submission. Fix your thoughts on him, whether you speak or keep quiet. Watch for his every move.

Should you find that, even then, your mind has wandered, don't panic. To worry about it, and make a great fuss, just serves to heighten the problem and distract the mind still further. Quietly and calmly the will must reassert itself, briefly confessing the fault and then focusing the thoughts again on God. If you persevere at this—no matter if it happens twenty times in ten minutes—God will take pity on you, the distractions will become less, the mind will learn that it has a master in the will.

One way to improve mental concentration during prayer is to improve it at other times as well. It is a healthy exercise to practice control over wandering thoughts and day dreams through the day. Our minds should be constantly in the presence of God, and a conscious act of submission of our thoughts to him at intervals during the day will accustom us to center all our thoughts and desires on him. Prayer is not different from the other ingredients of living: it is really a concentrating and distilling of them before God. Our lives should be lived out before him—and if they are, then our times of prayer will not be so disastrously besieged by wandering and distracting thoughts.

I hope this helps. Above all, don't be

discouraged. The heart is deceitful above all things, but God understands our frailty . . . he remembers that we are "only dust".

In Christ,
LAURIE

14 PUT YOUR HEART WITH YOUR TREASURE

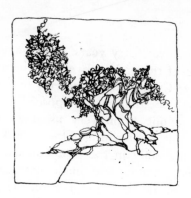

My dear John,
Would you pass on the enclosed note to Miss
Bennett? She wrote me a long letter, full of
questions and requests for advice, but I do
not have her address, so I'm asking you to act
as my mailman.

Miss Bennett seems to me to have excellent
intentions, but little patience. She tries to run
faster than grace. I have tried to tell her, very
gently, that one does not become holy all at
once, whatever some enthusiastic Christians
may say. We must learn to walk before we can
run.

Let me know how she gets on, from time
to time, won't you? I'm sure she will be
fervent, but hope she will also be obedient.

After all, our chief ambition in life should
be to please God, and we can only do that by
obeying him. Everything else is folly and
unreality. You and I have walked with him,

John, for over forty years. Have we made the best use of them? Have we used them to love and serve God, who in his mercy has called us to himself for that very purpose? For myself, I must admit I am very ashamed when I contrast his wonderful goodness and kindness to me, not only in the past but also today, with my grudging and inadequate love and service, and my slow progress on the path to "the perfect man".

Well, all is not lost. We have a little time left, by his mercy. It isn't too late for us to make up for lost time and return to God, the "Father of mercies", who is always ready to welcome us back. It isn't too late to re-nounce, for love of him, all that is not consistent with that love, and to train our minds to think of him constantly. I have no doubt that, if we do, the results will exceed our wildest hopes.

As I see it, John, we cannot even hope to escape the spiritual dangers that surround us in the modern world without the actual and *continual* help and grace of God. Without it, we can do nothing but sin. With it, we can do "all things". So—let's pray for his grace continually.

Yet, how can we pray to him without being with him, in his presence? And how can we be with him without thinking of him often? And how can we often think of him unless we form a habit of doing so? These things don't just happen!

I know what you are thinking to yourself as you read this—"Dear old Laurie, back on his hobby horse again!" Well, I admit it, I do harp on it, but only because it's true—this is the best, and easiest, and most effective method I know of cultivating the presence of God. I have used it for many years, and can only recommend it to everybody else.

After all, we must know someone before we can love them. In order to know God, we must think of him. And when we think of him, our love will grow, because our hearts will be where our treasure is.

Forgive me for playing an old record again and again! Yet you know how much this means to me, and how anxious I am that everybody should share in it.

Yours, in him,
LAURIE

15 PRIORITIES

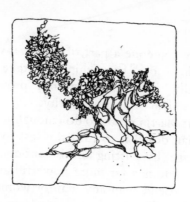

Dear Philip and Mary,
You really put me on the spot! I've delayed writing to your friend Martin all week, and have only got down to it now because I simply could not refuse a request from such old and dear friends as you. I'm enclosing a letter to him—would you address the envelope and forward it to him? You didn't give me his address. I am delighted to know of your own trust and confidence in God. It's a fact, isn't it, that we just can't have too much of so good and faithful a friend, who will never let us down—in this world, or the next.

Which brings me to Martin's problem. I can quite understand how upset he is over the way his human friend has let him down. Our Lord, too, knew what it was to be forsaken by his friends when he needed them most. It is a common enough human experience, because fallen men and women *are* unreliable.

We give someone a part of ourselves when we give them our friendship. We take a risk. Naturally, it hurts when they prove to be fickle, selfish or untrustworthy.

What Martin needs to do (though it is easier said than done) is to turn this loss to his own advantage, by putting all his confidence again in *God*. He is a far more powerful and more reliable friend than any man or woman. But, more than that, he changes our circumstances as he pleases. It may well be that he has another human friend for Martin, far better and more reliable than the one he has lost.

Perhaps Martin was *too* attached to his friend. It is right to love our friends, of course—but without trespassing on the love of God, which must take first place.

We can, in fact, learn a great deal about love of God from the way we treat our friends. For example, it would be very discourteous to invite a friend to our home and then leave him to sit alone in a corner while we go ahead with our own activities, ignoring him completely. Yet that is what we do with God. We have invited him, in his Son, to enter our hearts and live there—but often we neglect him, almost forgetting that he is there at all, so distracted are we by other things and other people.

The Christian's biggest most important job on earth is to live and die with the Lord. He can hardly do that if the slightest diversion drives all thoughts of God out of his mind. It is all a question of priorities, really.

Yours in the Lord,
LAURIE

16 SWEETNESS IN SUFFERING

Mrs. Marion Jones,
Surgical Ward
Massachusetts General Hospital

Dear Marion,
I have had you on my mind ever since our
fellowship meeting at lunch time today, when
Lois told us of your condition and several of
your friends prayed very movingly for your
recovery, or the relief of your pain. I hope
you will forgive my writing to you, but I
believe God wants me to do this and I can get
no peace of mind until I do his will.

You see, I could not really and truly join in
their prayers for you—not that I doubt either
their sincerity or their faith, and certainly not
that I am indifferent to your suffering, but
because I have learnt, through the small
burdens of pain that I have had to bear, a
different and (dare I suggest) a better way to

please God in times of illness.

I have been thinking how to say this. It is simply that I would rather we concentrated our prayers upon *you*, rather than your suffering. Let me explain.

I am sure you accept the fact that God has permitted you to suffer in this way. If he is truly *King* then this illness could not have come to you against his will. I believe (with the Epistle to the Hebrews, chapter twelve) that such things come to us from the hand of God, as a means which he uses to make us more completely his, and that rightly accepted and borne they bring great sweetness and consolation into our lives. This illness is not, then, an enemy to be fought, but an ally in the spiritual warfare to be gladly received and used.

So take strength from this: Christ holds you fastened to this cross; and Christ will release you from it when he thinks fit. In either case, it is obviously better to be held by him—on or off a cross—than to be apart from him.

Of course, you can't expect those who do not believe in God to see things in this way. You cannot ask an unbeliever to suffer as a Christian. He considers illness as an enemy of life and nature, and finds nothing in it but grief and distress. The Christian, however, sees it as coming from the hands of God. This is the crucial difference.

I hope you can discover for yourself that God is often—at least, in some sense—nearer to us in sickness than in health. To put all our hope and faith into *recovery* is almost like saying we want to have less of him. Instead, we should put our faith and hope *in him*. After all, even the medical treatment you receive and the drugs you are given will only succeed so far as he permits. Perhaps he is reserving your complete cure to himself, and waiting only for you to commit yourself into his hands without question.

I expect you are saying to yourself— "That's all right for *him*." But, truthfully, however happy you may think I am at this moment, I envy you. To suffer *with my God* is not pain, but paradise. To "enjoy myself" without him would be hell. I must, very shortly (weeks, months, years—who knows?) go to God. What comforts me here and now is that I can see him and know him by faith. But then I shall believe no more. I shall *see*. So—as St. Paul himself put it—"for me to live is Christ, and to die is gain." Anything—life, joy, pain, death—that brings me nearer to him cannot be bad.

Keep close to God. I shall ask him to be with you.

Yours, because his,
LAURIE

17 The Offering of Pain

Mrs. Marion Jones,
Surgical Ward
Massachusetts General Hospital

My dear Marion,
I have had you very much in my thoughts and
prayers since I last wrote to you a couple of
weeks ago. I have a little idea of how much
you must be suffering, and I want you to
know that what I did *not* mean that suffering
was unimportant or easily borne, even with
God's help. What I was trying to say was that
if we are accustomed to live in the presence of
God, and if we believe that everything that
comes to us comes with his permission, then
those two facts will help to alleviate our
suffering. God often permits us to suffer a
little, to lead us on to maturity, and to drive
us into his arms.

So, offer him your pains. They come from

him, or by his permission, so turn them into an offering to lay at his feet—his will for you accepted and carried through. Ask him for the strength you will need to bear them. And, above all, continually lift your thoughts away from the pain you feel and towards him, who loves you as a Father his favorite child. God has many ways of drawing us to himself. Sometimes his way is to hide himself from us for a time. It is then, most of all, that faith, and faith *only,* will support us and give a firm foundation to our confidence in him.

I have no idea what God may have in store for me, of pleasure or of pain. All I know is—and sometimes it almost makes me feel guilty—that in a world where suffering faces us on every side, I, who deserve only to be punished by God, feel such a continual joy in him that at times I can hardly stop myself shouting and rejoicing from the roof-tops!

Dear Marion, I would willingly ask God for a part of your pain, if that would help—but I know my weakness, and know that without his continual presence I should be unable to bear it. But I also know that he has promised never to leave me. Let us resolve never to leave him. Let us live and die in his presence.

Pray for me as I promise to pray for you.

Yours in him,
LAURIE

18 IN THE HANDS OF GOD

Mrs. Marion Jones
Surgical Ward
Massachusetts General Hospital

My dear Marion,
It hurts me to see you suffer. Since I saw you last week, I have had you constantly in my thoughts and in my prayers. The only relief I can find is to reassure myself that God must love you very much to permit you to suffer so much. He must also be very confident of your love for him. "The Lord disciplines those whom he *loves* . . . ."

However, I have another particular reason for writing. You remember we were talking last week about "putting God to the test"— the danger of asking God to do miraculously what we are well able to do, in his strength, without a miracle. We were especially talking about healing, and I argued that it was right to use human medicine and medical skills, because they, too, were given by God, rather than seek a sort of spiritual short-cut by asking for direct divine healing.

But as I have thought and prayed about you, I have come to feeling that the moment is now passed when you could be expected to rely on ordinary medical care. You know this, so it is not cruel to put it into words: humanly speaking, your case is hopeless. You have endured for months the often painful investigations and treatments prescribed by your doctors. You have had surgery, chemotherapy, cobalt therapy and just about everything else—and you have accepted it all patiently, and co-operated with those who have taken care of you.

But you are no better. In fact, as you yourself realize, you are getting weaker every day.

In such circumstances, I wonder whether it might not be right for you to have a talk with your doctor, and say to him that you appreciate very much all that has been done for you, and the thought and devotion that has gone into your treatment, but, as it doesn't seem to be achieving anything, you would now prefer to be left in the hands of God. It would not, I'm sure, be "tempting God" to resign yourself with perfect trust into his hands, for healing, if that is his will; or for a quiet and peaceful path into his presence, if that is what he desires for you.

I do not mean, of course, that you should reject all medical care, or that such a course rules out your receiving drugs or other treatment which will lessen your pain. I simply mean that the moment may have come when your chief concern should cease to be human remedies, and start to be a total and trusting dependence on the providence of God. That is not to say that you have not been trusting him all along. But you have, up to now, been looking for him to help you *through human agents* (your doctors and nurses). Now, perhaps, he wants you to expect everything *from him.* In a sense, this is simply to make a virtue out of a necessity. Human help—skillful and dedicated though it be—cannot meet your needs. Turn, then, to God, and comfort yourself with him, the only Physician who fully understands and can completely cure every sickness of body and spirit.

I know it is hard to pray for strength to bear pain, rather than for the pain to be taken away. But love sweetens pain—think of a mother in childbirth. And when one loves God, and feels his warm answering love, pain *is* sweetened. He loves us beyond our wildest imagination. Let him prove his promises.

Always yours in our Lord,
LAURIE

19 heaven's threshold

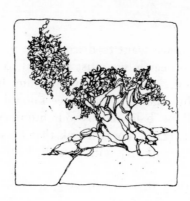

Mrs. Marion Jones
Surgical Ward
Massachusetts General Hospital

My dear Marion,
I was so glad to hear from you, though your letter took rather a long time to reach me! Since I saw you I've been rather ill myself, and had the opportunity to test the advice I had been giving you. In fact, I think I can say I've been "at death's door" once or twice recently—and, as I expected, never felt nearer God than when standing on the threshold of heaven.

I am so thankful to God for the news that you are feeling better and that he has drawn nearer to you as you have drawn nearer to him. I have always believed, and am more sure than ever now, that it is paradise to suffer with him, but hell to be at ease without him.

So that, if we want to discover the peace of paradise on earth, we must get used to living in constant communication with him. In this relationship the familiarity (we know him so well) will be balanced by our humility (because it is staggering to think that *he* should want to be with *us*), with love the keynote of it all.

More than that, we must guard our affections, like a faithful husband or wife, keeping them for him and making sure that we are not seduced by any earthly distraction. We must convert the inner sanctuary of our affections into a spiritual temple where he is constantly worshipped. And we must check ourselves— our actions, attitudes and words—continually, to see that we are not displeasing him. If we do these things, heaven is already here, and suffering is robbed of its bitter bite.

I realize that it is difficult, at least at first, to follow this path. Our instinct is to shrink from pain and suffering—and hide ourselves from God. The core of the difficulty, however, is not the presence of pain, but the absence of *faith*. We find it very hard to believe that God knows all, and therefore that what he plans for us is best. We prefer to follow our fallen reason, or our own defective sight. But "we walk by faith, not by sight".[1] What we can see, and what we can understand is very, very limited. God knows and sees *all*.

So, although it *is* difficult, it is not impossible. I have proved that. God never refuses his grace to those who ask for his help sincerely—and the chief part of that grace is the gift of faith to trust him. Knock at his door, and keep on knocking—and I promise you that in his own good time God will open to you and give you everything that he has been waiting to give you for many years.

I am at his door now, and expecting to see him at any moment. Pray for me, Marion, as I do for you.

LAURIE

[1] 2 Corinthians 5:7.

20   ONE SIMPLE ACT

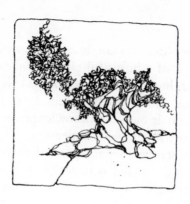

Mrs. Marion Jones
Surgical Ward
Massachusetts General Hospital

My dear Marion,
God knows what we really need, and all he
does is for the best. If only we could grasp
how much he loves us, we should be more
ready to receive with trusting joy both the
bitter and the sweet from his hand. All we
must know is that it comes from him . . . and
this he has assured us. Pain is only intolerable
when seen in a distorted light. But when we
know it is the hand of a loving God that
shapes it all, and that it is our Father who
gives us the cup of sorrow to drink, there is
no distortion and so no unbearable burden.

  We should concentrate on knowing God.
The more we know him, the more we shall
long to know him better. Love without

knowledge (like a man infatuated with the photograph of a beautiful girl) is shallow and superficial; but the deeper our knowledge, the deeper and more satisfying our love. If our love of God is based on knowledge, we shall love him equally in pain or pleasure.

Many Christians seem to feel that the way to get "near" to God is to seek experience of him—special gifts and sensations of the Holy Spirit. But it seems to me that such experiences, however moving, cannot bring us as near God as faith does in one simple act! After all, he is not far away. He is *within* us. We have no need to look for him anywhere else. Wouldn't it be regarded as foolish, and even wrong, to go off in search of the good, when the best is being offered to us?

So let us seek the best, and the best is his presence with us all day long. Let us reject all substitutes for this. If we take only one hesitant step towards him, he will come to meet us.

Forgive me—I didn't mean to preach a sermon! I'm delighted to hear of the way God has comforted and relieved you. To him be the thanks and the glory.

For my part, I hope to have the joy of seeing him any day now. Let us pray for one another.

Yours in the Lord,
LAURIE

21 GOD IS OUR GOAL

A few days after writing that last letter to Marion Jones, Brother Lawrence was taken seriously ill, and within a week he had died. So ended a life which, though carried on in humble circumstances and completely without publicity, was exceptional for its honesty, quality and knowledge of God. Just before he retired from the hospital S.D. kitchen, a member of our fellowship asked Laurie to sum up what his faith meant in terms of his daily work. This was his reply.

"You all know that soon after my conversion at the age of eighteen I set myself to make God the goal of all my thoughts and desires. To help towards this, I spent the hours appointed in our Community for private prayer thinking of God, so as to convince my mind of his real and actual existence and let that truth impress itself deeply on my heart. I did this, let me say, not by elaborate intellectual processes (which would be beyond me), nor by complicated schemes of meditation, but by opening my mind and then my heart to the light of faith. The result of this, as I have often tried to explain, was an overwhelming sense of the reality of God's presence, and I resolved never to forget him or neglect him again. In fact, I have often failed; but he always welcomes me back again when I confess my failure and turn once more to him.

"On a normal, working day, I would try to fill my waking mind with thoughts of God—in his infinite power, and in his personality. The Bible often began my thinking, and prayer always filled this out and made it personal to me.

"So, by the time I set off to work, I had already been in God's presence for an hour or so—not just on my knees, you must understand, but while I had been shaving and eating my breakfast, too.

"When I got to the kitchen I would check on the day's menus, assignments, special diets, delivery schedules and so on. Then, having got a picture of the day's work, I would briefly but deliberately commit it to God. I often used the same prayer:

" 'O my God, you are always with me. Since I must now, in obedience to your will for me, apply my mind to my day's work, grant me the grace I shall need to continue through it in your presence. Help me to do this work to your glory. Receive it as a spiritual offering. And let my desire be only to please you.'

"Then, as the day's routine began, I would know that I was as near God, and he as near me, as if I could have seen him there with my physical eyes.

"At the end of the day I would stop to think about how it had gone. If things had gone well, both in my work and in my consciousness of God, I would give him thanks. If it had not gone well, I would ask his forgiveness and, without allowing myself to become discouraged by failure, would set my mind right again and turn once more to thinking of God as if I had never stopped. So I can honestly say that, through years of practice, I have come to a condition where it would be as difficult for me not to think of God, as it used to be to get into the habit of doing so."

Not surprisingly, in view of the tremendous blessing Laurie obtained from his walk with God, he would often urge the rest of us to seek him in the same kind of way. This might have been embarrassing or annoying. But in fact his own life was a stronger argument for his cause than any words he could find. Just to look at him was to be convinced—his face radiated joy and calmness, no matter how hectic the day.

In fact, it was this that impressed people most of all about him. The Special Diets kitchen was often very busy, and usually under-staffed. The phone seemed to ring incessantly, and yet people expected the meals to arrive on the wards at the exact time scheduled. But, in the busiest moments, with noise, heat and tempers getting a bit frayed at the edges, Laurie remained calm—and close to God.

It wasn't that he wandered through it all with a sort of distant, "spiritual" look on his face, remote from us lesser mortals. That would be a hopelessly wrong picture. It was just that panic (on the one hand) or laziness (on the other) were totally foreign to him. He was serving God, and that would be best done by being calm, composed . . . and hard-working. He saw no hint of contradiction in those attitudes.

"After all," he once said to me, "the times when I am working and the times when I am praying are no different in *kind*. In the noise and clutter of the kitchen, with half a dozen people screaming for different things at once, I can possess the peace of God, and know the God of peace, as truly as if I were on my knees at the altar rail."